Age of Aquarius

Collected Poems 1981-2016

Dianne Borsenik

Almost all of the poems in Age of Aquarius *have appeared in various journals, anthologies, newspapers, magazines, and chapbooks during the thirty-five year span between 1981 and 2016. Some poems appear here in print for the first time since their original publication.*

With deep gratitude to John Burroughs for publishing this collection.

With deep gratitude to all those who have published and supported my work during the thirty-five years represented here.

With love and special thanks to my "biggest fan," my husband James, for his unfaltering encouragement and support.

—Dianne Borsenik, March 2016

Age of Aquarius: Collected Poems 1981 – 2016

© 2016 by Dianne Borsenik
dianneborsenik.com
all rights reserved by the author

Crisis Chronicles #83
ISBN: 978-1-940996-34-9
published 20 March 2016
1st edition, 4th printing, 20 copies

Crisis Chronicles Press
John Burroughs, editor/publisher
3431 George Avenue
Parma, Ohio 44134

crisischronicles.com
ccpress.blogspot.com
facebook.com/crisischroniclespress

When the moon is in the 7th House and Jupiter aligns with Mars, then peace will guide the planets and love will steer the stars....

This is the dawning of the Age of Aquarius

"Aquarius / Let the Sun Shine In"
— The 5th Dimension

Contents

1.......Age of Aquarius
2.......Disco
3.......Cinco de Mayo Moon
4.......Fortune Cookie
6.......Lovechild
7.......Elemental
8.......Tie-Dye
9.......When October's Throat Is Cut to Celebrate Samhain
10.....Fire
11.....Water
12.....Thirst
13.....Licking Winter
14.....Greenheart
16.....Hairy Situation
17.....Hipster
18.....Hippie Chick, Baby
19.....Back That Thang Up
20.....Rocker
21.....Reading Palms
22.....Drumming Circle
23.....Blue Moon
24.....Where the Sky Goes
25.....Import
26.....Lost
27.....Seeds
28.....Sacrifice and Broken Fevers
29.....In a Bar, the Basement, a Microphone, and Poets
30.....BeatStreet Cleveland
31.....Let's Get It On
32.....Tribe
33.....Everybody Must Get Stoned
34.....Bad, Inc.
35.....Stopping by Bar on a Rainy Evening
36.....Back to the Pack
41.....Incontinence
42.....NetWork
44.....Red Stilettos
45.....Kicking It
46.....Two Bottles
48.....Family Tree
50.....Flower Power
51.....One Peachy Day
52.....Cravings
54.....One Small Step
57.....Black and White
58.....Cary Grant Walks
59.....Frank Sinatra Sighs

60.....Soul Custody
61.....Serious Moonlight
62.....Trick Whore Treat
63.....Merrily, Merrily
64.....Easter/West
66.....Baby Needs a New Pair of Wings
67.....Night Ballet
68.....Black Mass
70.....Purdah
71.....Daisy Chain
72.....Countdown
73.....Blue Heart
74.....All I Want Is to Leave
75.....Brother, Can You Spare a Dime
76.....Check Out
78.....Few Dollar Man
80.....Cleveland Spelled Backwards Is
82.....Casting Call
85.....Happy Hour
86.....Got Soul?
89.....Thaumaturgy
90.....Frankie's Too Cool
92.....Bohemian Vendetta
93.....Going Braless
94.....Conscientious Objector
96.....Serious Flannel
97.....Cupid
98.....Her First Time
99.....Story Book
100....Psalm
101....In This Desert
102....Each Stroke a Promise
103....Wood I Love You
104....Summer and Smoke
105....Making Scents
106....Sugar, Spice and Everything Twice
108....You Are You
109...Butterfly
110...These Places
111...Wet
112...Pink Hell
114...Bufo Alvarius
115...Dark Shadow
116...The Nightmare Spinners
118...Wraiths
119...Fusion
120...Learning the Form
121...Mutability
122...Jawbone
124...Communication Breakdown

126...Mother Tongue
131....Champagne Dance
132....HardDrive/SoftWear
134....QRU
135....Antiphon for Winter Solstice
136....Flow
137....Día de los Muertes
138....Pools of–
139...The View

141...Acknowledgments

Age of Aquarius

In this forest
of a different god,
where angels' eyes
are closed and kissed,
stained glass walls
will not be missed.

Ash and oak drink in
the sacred dawn,
their branches stippled
by the rain.
Silver fingers trace
the veins

of flower children,
whisper patterns
to them in the womb.
Stars give birth,
constellations dance,
and earth

returns a joyous
music to her
fields. Songs long
dormant now explode,
flinging wide
the change encoded

in the matrix
of the soul. Rejoice!
as we forgive us
of our sins.
This is where
it all begins.

Disco

—after the Prayer Series by Hui-Chu Ying

Earth. Air. Fire. Water.
These are sequins

in the eternal disco.
Moon's mirrored ball spins

jitterbug flakes
to bathe our Dance.

Before earth, water.
Before water, air.

Before air, fire.
Before fire, glittering stardust.

We, electric, slide
into the future.

We wear our arias
like diamonds.

Cinco de Mayo Moon

cinco de mayo moon
pale pink piñata moon
hanging low
marshmallow moon
hostess sno ball moon
plump sofa cushion moon
lounging on the horizon
spotlight moon
punching a hole in the night
magician moon
making us look
tango moon
dancing with the stars
tracing giant arcs with its toe
siren moon
luring us to luna pier
inviting us to jump in
la seducción de la luna

Fortune Cookie

Fortune
smile upon this
blue-eyed, tie-dyed
cloudy-skied
wild child
I beseech you
reach out your rabbit foot luck
and caress me
stroke me, grope me, poke me
brush me, bless me
with upturned trunks of pluck
and plenty
pour your
shamrocks, acorns, clover
over me
show me mercy
I implore you
send me
sunshine
good times
pay me some mind
you've played at being blind
too long
and it's wrong to ignore
your acolyte this way

Fortune
I invoke you
show your power
shower me with
happiness
cast your Ganesh gaze
upon me, Buddha me
with scraps of hope
wrapped up in cookie dough
raise my chances like
Jesus raised the dead
cross my heart

anoint my forehead
talk to me of salt
thrown over the shoulder
and sharp knocks on wood
I'll walk
your pagan ways
your numbers, runes, die
amulets and shuffled cards
I'll thank my lucky stars
and be at your command
own me, charm me
take me by the hand
let no misfortune
harm me
lead me to your
promised land

O Fortune, I beg you
please
don't leave me
in the dust
dole it out
a little at a time
if you must
but Fortune, please

please
oh baby
please
don't let my horseshoe
rust

Lovechild

make incense from the flowers
dance naked in the light
weave a blanket
fringed with stars
to cover you at night
breathe kisses to the morning
braid songs into your hair
blow a wish
on feathered spores
that surf the curls of air
and if a storm
should hurt you
pour honey on the pain
chase the clouds
and catch them
then laugh!
and drink the rain

Elemental

touch bare feet
to the earth
and don't let go
feel it throb
like a living prayer
sway the dance
of confetti fireflies
let your fingers
weave the air
wear the night
like a thin
silk jacket
pluck the stars
for a torch
and a flame
follow your heart
to the cradle
of life
and the ocean
will give you
your name

Tie-Dye

incense evening
    washed
        by autumn
            hung to dry
                sun-shed colors
        plum and crimson
      spilled and smearing
stain the sky

When October's Throat Is Cut to Celebrate Samhain

darkness spilling
from the wounded sky

and the warm gush
of crimson leaves...

guillotine wind
has struck again

Fire

—West Virginia, 2012

so much
fog rising from
these mountains, it looks as
if the rain is extinguishing
fires

Water

—Florida, 2012

water
upon water
makes its own strange beauty
torrential rain in waves, on waves
wet Zen

Thirst

Her sky is saried in silks of palest blue,
in rose and lavender shot through with golden
thread; and in her eyes are the mornings
of a thousand namastes. Her fingers, curled
into bowls, carry whispers of pain and promise,
all she knew of love. Lemonscent trails
behind her as she walks, thyme crushed
by her footsteps in a dance of impatience,
and when she opens her cherried lips to sing
the Saraswati Vandana, each syllable
is a snowflake melting its way to a distant star.

Licking Winter

could berry juice
coax your hard mouth
to fall in love

could sweet yellow light
relax your nature

could windsong cut
between the thick vines
of your wild sanctuary

could the colors of eden
murmur to your shade
and root out its harsh night

listen to the rustle

it's as if all things
moist and sacred
are flowering in stone

Greenheart

—*to Robert Anthony Plant*

If it should rain
today, then walk
with me. We'll shed
our clothes and slip
between the trees,
hand in hand and
skin to skin, lost
in a landscape
of pagan green,
where thunder beats
its *bodhrán* drum,
and silvered leaves
become a tambourine.

And if the sun
should shine today,
then dance with me.
We'll bare our feet
and find the beat
within our hearts,
stand lip to lip
and speak in tongues,
two of a kind,
enraptured by
the blazing heat
that shapes our world,
our bodies intertwined.

And if the night
should start to fall
and stars appear,
then sleep with me.
We'll wrap our arms
around the moon
and hug it close;
transcending time,

anointed by
the stuff of dreams,
the two of us
becoming one,
supernal where we lie.

Hairy Situation

Here's the thing—since my teen years, I've had
An abiding weakness for long hair.
I mean long hair on men, of course. Think…
Robert Plant, in his heyday with Led Zeppelin.
Yeah, I love a big mane of hair tossed over the
Shoulders and cascading down the back.
If you've never kissed with your fingers
Tangled in a man's long hair, you don't know the
Unbridled glory of unbound, unbraided, free-flowing
Aphrodisiacal keratin filaments sticking to your lips,
Teasing your bare skin, tiny silken strands tickling your
Ivories and making your entire body burst into song!
Of course, I have a hairy situation here…my husband's
Noggin's been bald for years. Dreaming's free, isn't it?

Hipster

Having experienced that year my 40th birthday,
I was bumming quite a bit. But then Robert
Plant blew me a kiss from the Cleveland
Stage during a concert, and oh! I was a
Teenager again, a Ginsberg bursting with the bright
Energy of a black-clad, beatnik hipster grooving,
Reciting "Howl" at the top of her lungs, triumphant!

Hippie Chick, Baby

Happiest I've ever been?
I'm not sure I can
Pick just one moment out of the sparkling
Panoply of days I've had.
I can tell you that being an
Embryonic hippie chick back in the day was a
Certifiably groovy way to start. I wore
Headbands and huarache sandals,
Imagined myself levitating the Pentagon, going to
Concerts, peace marches, love-ins. I just
Knew it was a special, magical time like no other.
But I was too young for college, for Woodstock,
And by the time I was old enough, the 60s
Boat had sailed. Still, I can claim the 60s experience.
You'll never be able to take the hippie out of me.

Back That Thang Up*

Baby got back,
And baby got front, too.
Call me bird or chick, gal or girl,
Know that I am woman, with all
The desires and dreams of someone
Half my age. Years don't matter;
After all is said and done, it's
The mind that determines libido.
This baby's motor is running at
High speed, and I'm racing flat-out
Against the Grim Reaper.
Nothing's going to hold me back. I'm
Going to want to hear "back that thang
Up, you're a fine motherfucker" until
Placed in the oven at the crematorium.

*incorporates lyrics by Juvenile, Mannie Fresh, and Lil Wayne

19

Rocker

—Ohio, 2012

going
through the Rock Hall
of Fame, realizing
that I am a museum piece
as well

Reading Palms

Red again. What a relief!
Every four weeks like clockwork I keep my
Appointment with Karen and get my hair re-
Dyed to cover up the gray. Oh,
I'm totally comfortable with my age,
Now that I'm here. I worked hard for it, and I'm
Going to get every senior discount coming to me.
Palm readers will tell you what they see in
A line or notch, but I can predict my own future with a
Lot more accuracy: I'm going to revel in these years,
Make new challenges for myself and meet them,
See this party through to the end, refuse to fade, to
                                                    disappear.

Drumming Circle

in this circle
scented grasses
mixed with innocent
expression
met with destiny
and longing
find the moment
of the blessing
with stone turning
from its silence
where the distance
is uncertain
and the stars contain
the measure
and the magic
of a woman
clad in moonlight
chanting mystic
with the proper
intonation
with investment
in perception
woaded shadows
bend to listen
guided by a purple
dawning
past and future
in collision
celebrating
summer's secrets
solstice brings
a new
religion

Blue Moon

lunar fingers
elongated
bone-white
penetrate
cloud curtain
slip through
crawl across
scarred wax
frozen landscape
silent night

mocking
star-lacquered
pickpocket
fingers dip
into cracks
raise gooseflesh
trail snail
slime shadows
diaphanous
lunatic fringe

forever dead
fingers draw
chalk outlines
steal passage
on blackwater
broadcast
syllables
of lust
naked longing
high tide

Where the Sky Goes

—after "Wish Flying Farther and Higher"
by Bich Tiên Nguyễn Ngọc

above the blue
lake of clouds,
climbing off the earth
and over the moon,
a long way out, following
time's dark wonder

into that black sea
of glowing answers,
ancient and quiet
and all the colors
of imagining,
starshine thick
like a winter storm

our secret wishes fly
never knowing
why they are born,
bigger than we
can begin to understand

Import

—*Tres Versing the Panda, Cleveland, OH, 2009*

He is speaking to me in a language
that I do not know.

His mouth is forming sounds
that I cannot understand,

although it pleasures my ears
to hear them. I can make no sense

of these strange words, so I concentrate
instead on the way he moves his

fingers in time with the rise and fall
of his emphasis and inflection,

the shine of the lamplight as it limns
the lock of hair that falls over one eye.

I find myself falling into the cracks
between his word-sounds, losing

touch with the reality of vowels and
consonants, sibilants and gutturals,

the sweet lisps of meaning. What is
meaning, anyway, but one man's

declaration of absolute, no room for
gray, or the tickle of dandelion spores,

each tiny parachute another permutation
in the melody of life.

Lost

give me quiet turquoise moments
Lethe and prayer
resolution of my shattered dreams
restoration of my tattered control
give me meditations enough
to ease the ills of my mortality
give me back my virginal innocence
make the opaque go crystal again

for I am lost in this uncertain
curtained way of maze and tryst,
of trusts betrayed and light gone dark
I cannot find myself inside
the twisted strands of DNA and doubt
I'm caught between the spectral bands
of black and white, where everything
I thought I knew is somehow wrong,
and lost

so give me quiet turquoise moments
Lethe and prayer
absolution for unremembered sins
abrogation where immutability begins
let balance and belief find rebirth
in the frozen cobalt ashes of my eyes
heal my aura, ego, id, and soul
let me feel a new reality

Seeds

Yesterday, and I'm talking distant past here,
Oracles might have directed
Us differently, might have
Voiced concerns about stability and
Events occurring naturally, might have
Given us advice to keep
Our heads down and stay out of
Trouble, just to work
Toward feeding our families and building
Our homes and surviving our lives. Minor
Changes would have occurred in common, everyday
Happenings of birth, marriage, death:
All major changes would have involved the
Negative aspects of invasion, displacement, war.
Given the times, any change would have been scary
Enough. Now, though, with each passing
Year, the world becomes smaller, and
Our facility with technology helps move
Us toward a universal consciousness. It's our
Responsibility to foster change, to
Encourage growth, to protest the
Vile practices of destroying the environment,
Imprisoning the innocent, denying the
Legal right of marriage to those in love.
With our hearts wide open, we need to heed the call,
Acknowledge distress and address the wrongs,
Yes, and to know that the earth is fertile for those
Sprouts of enlightenment, those crops of compassion.
Believe, become, be strong, and be ready to take
Action. You must
Be the change
You want to *seed* in the world.

Sacrifice and Broken Fevers

Remember when candy
was a god thing
how you listened to its voice,
desired to know its magic,
celebrated caramel secrets,
explored every sacred center?
Could there have beat
a more trusting heart?
But then the dark angel
of change worked his lie,
ghosted from hand to eye,
killed that wild bone
of dazzle.

If you put yourself
in the smoke,
make peace with the lingering
fires, blaze harder
than those hot mornings,
You will learn to heal.
Ask poetry:
it says "Come,
you can drink my melted smiles;
eat of me, and
be free."

In a Bar, the Basement, a Microphone, and Poets

—Annabell's Bar and Lounge, Akron, OH, 01/16/16

Ave, ave, cathedral of drink, holy temple of fizz,
bubble and clink, of bourbon, of whiskey,
cognac, rum, tequila, of vodka and XX,
dram, draft, glass, bottle, shot, pint, brew,
every sip a communion sanctioned by dot gov,
Father Bartender blessing me, blessing you,
giving us all another chance to forget
how tomorrow might play out, what our chances
in this crazy game of life might be, and in the corner,
juices pulsing down the throat of the mic, Hpnotiq,
kicking ass, kneecapping the competition, flip,
laughing, unrepentant, irreverent, a literary mojo
more intoxicating than any proof alcohol, more than—

BeatStreet Cleveland

—Barking Spider, Cleveland, OH, 2015

BeatStreet Cleveland!
Where the rubber hits the road
and the road rises to meet it,
where blue collar and blue blood
come together to feast
on the blue mimeograph
milk of poetry,
to follow in the footsteps of levy
and Hughes, Crane and Thompson,
to create a happening, a be-in,
a revolution of new words.
BeatStreet Cleveland!
Where blue sky blends with blue Erie
and blue Erie with blue evening
and blue evening with the sweet blue
music of the cosmos, our city spinning
and spinning, all of us
a dot on the terrestrial top,
centrifugal force pulling us into the future,
our bodies containing multitudes,
containing galaxies, the horizon
wide open, possibilities pouring
from the clouds like rain.
BeatStreet Cleveland!
Where we run across her concrete,
splash through her wet neon, laughing,
where we don't know the meaning of
can't make it happen.

Let's Get It On!

—*Snoetry 5, Erie, PA 2015*

"Follow your inner moonlight; don't hide the madness."
—*Allen Ginsberg, excerpt from* On Being a Writer, *Writer's Digest Books 1989*

It's a Happening, baby, a right-on Be-In, a wide-eyed wonder, a thunderclap amen, a groove, a movement, a goodbye to yesterday and a shout out to tomorrow, so get those hands in the air, get those feet stomping and shake those moneymakers—it's kid-in-the-candy-store time, it's an all-day humdinger, it's driving a go-to-hell red Mustang with the top down, let's get it on, and light 'em if you got 'em kind of thing.

It's a sassy grass green string of moments in a soft-focus camera lens, so let's get going, let's get funky, let's get down and dirty and clean the clocks of this sleepy old town; let's bust out (not rust out), slow time, blow minds, find the flow and go wild, howl happy and rap madly.

It's a Happening, baby, and we're here to stir the pot, dot the I's and cross the T's, grease the wheels and feel the please and spank you—it's time to rhumba the rhyme, twerk the stanzas, macarena the metaphors and shimmy the similes! Time to look alive, feel the shine, the sizzle, the spark, the snap, the bling, the poetry—so bring it and swing it, let's get it on, and Welcome to Snoetry!

Tribe

—Saturday, October 18, 2014
—Levy Fest, Cleveland, OH

next week they're coming they're gonna make landfall like an unruly hurricane in June like a tornado in Omaha like a pigskin over the goal line it's Cleveland it's Levy Fest they're gonna take over CSU the Spotted Owl and the Literary Café and they're gonna torch those joints it's east coast west coast baby a meeting of minds a gathering of the tribes a gangland rendezvous it's a murder of crows a shiver of sharks a troop of kangaroos kicking it with the homies kicking the roof off this outlaw town it's Cleveland it's Levy Fest it's a temporary moment of glory in a permanent collection of memorabilia it's popping a poetic cap in the city's ass and living to rap the story

Everybody Must Get Stoned

—Bob Dylan, "Rainy Day Women #12 & 35

it's time to turn it on time to rock hard rock solid rock
steady rock-a-bye baby time to rock out with your cock
out rock and roll rock around the clock throw away the
rocking chair and move it like you mean it time to rocket
to the moon to mars to a comet to an asteroid they're
just bigger rocks anyway don't take this time for granite

Bad, Inc.

I keep bad company my posse is wild at heart and hell-bent for feathered quills and 96 percent bright nothing stops our bad, inc. from taking what we want we ride roughshod over the rugged landscapes of keyboard and keypad sleep wrapped in blankets of scratchy thought we blaze trails range wide and howl songs of both victory and loss under a tombstone moon we wave our outlaw status like a flag swagger in armed to the teeth with daggered wit and feelings on our sleeves swallow shots of fresh blood we shoot off our mouths and take slugs in return spit out the bullets with a grin when my posse hits town we rob the past to give to the future we write crooked truth we make a mess as we kick through all those sawdust verses littering the floor we slam our empties on the counter shake our raw fists at convention we go to bed with our boots on get up before dawn our bad, inc. never lets down its guard never rides off into the sunset

Stopping by Bar on a Rainy Evening*

Stopped in at a bar on
The way home the
Other night. It was one of those
Post-reading nights, late, with me all
Pumped from performing at the mic, and
I didn't want to go home right away.
Never can go right to sleep, those nights. The
Gravity of the lights and conversations and
Brews drew me into the bar's bright orbit.
You know how I love a cold
Beer, and what it means for me to be
Able to sit and enjoy the drinking of it.
Reason enough, just to relax and reflect.
Only that's not all of it, not the only incentive.
No, I like the prerogative, the sanction, the
Authority, to drink, get intoxicated, or not, as
Regularly, or rarely, as the case may be.
After the restrictions of youth and religion, walking
Into a bar is pleasure in itself. I studied the blue
Neon, the bottles echoed in the mirror, the
Yellow spilling from the kitchen, the wood stains,
Even the rain streaking the black windows. This
Veneer of commercialized civilization satisfied my
Eyes, calmed my
Nameless disquiet. For the price of an
Inebriating, enlightening beverage or two, I found
Nirvana on the cheap. There's my choice of poison,
Going smiles before I sleep.

*with apologies to Robert Frost

Back to the Pack

*"We don't want you to come read your own poetry
any more...we'd like to have people come and read
classic poetry, Robert Frost and Emily Dickinson."*
—owner of a now defunct independent bookstore,
Lakewood, Ohio

"When poets are treated like dogs, they howl"
—Ferlinghetti, Poetry As Insurgent Art

You know who you are
And you know what you know
You howl, man
Really
Howl
You black wolf, you mad dog
You holy boy, Ginsby boy
Beatnik, dharma bum, con man
Loose among the unsuspecting
Flock, scattering the weak
Shattering the peace, shocking
The pop tarts and old farts
With a regular *sturm und drang*
Of furious words
A quasi-religious cant
A revolutionary rant
Hurtling from a darkness
So profound
It hurts to look at it

Bukowski knew this night
d. a. levy, Poe, Burroughs too
Morrison, Lennon, Hendrix
They all knew the taste
Of it, the embrace of it
All had their coarse fur ruffled
The wrong way by it
All raised hackles at slurs
All scrabbled for purchase
On the scree of ignorance

36

And rejection
All prowled and growled
And snapped at the heels
Of heels, feeling lost
And cast out
They knew

Cohen weeps with it, Reed
Walks on the wild side of it
Dylan, ah Dylan...he
Knows what's blowin' in
The wind, he smells that cold ash
Of bullshit and knows
Everyone has to fend
For himself. It's eat
Or be eaten, out here
In the sticks
Yeah, you know
You know who you are
And you know what you know
Although
Does anyone really know anyone
No one really knows
But we all know that "no"
Don't we?

Oh yeah, we know
We no
Another bourgeois bookstore
Door banged shut on
Our snouts
No
Another window of opportunity
Slammed
To keep our crass and
Degenerate influences
Out. We know
What we know, man
This game is fixed—you can look
Through the glass, Jack, but

Touch is nixed. No warm den,
No come on in, for
This wild pack. Huff
And puff all you want—some
Walls just won't
Blow down.

Is it getting hot in here?
451 degrees Fahrenheit, I'd
Say; all our good
Intentions going up in smoke
Yeah, I know what I know
And I'm feeling that choke
Collar slipping over
My head
I'm feeling
The wheeze
Of things not said
In my throat, feeling
The gag, the drag of
The chain, feeling my neck
Tighten to steel
Feeling my whole body
Straining
Against the leash

Hell, yeah, I want to eat
But I don't want to be spoon fed
They can keep their
Kibble and treats
And snacks and stacks
Of plastic classic pablum
Their fireside
Chats, their comfort zone
And monotone domesticity
And strokes
And pats on the back

I need a place
Where words and the wolves

Oh man, those bright dogs
Who write them
And right them
Are read, not dead

We know what we know
And we'll go where we go
Questioning
The status quo, testing
The limits
Of convention
Making a mess
Of their manicured
Lawns, their rose-colored
Gardens, making
That manure fly. We'll be
Restless, roaming, pesky
Sniffing around
Our noses pressed
To the cracks under
The doors
Always hungry
For more

But refusing the refuse
Stale crumbs
From the Conservative table
We may be outlaws but
We're not that unstable

It's time to howl, man
Really
Howl
You know who you are
And you know what you know
Come on, you bitches
Howl
Joplin howled, Plath howled
Doolittle barked at the moon
Come on, you dogs

You dark, wild
Wicked, willful
Wonderful wolves
Howwwl

Cry foul
Let's get alpha
On their asses, let's mark
Our territories with piss
And vinegar, heart's art
And mind's flight, let's fix them
With our yellow eyes and
Let loose
With our Howl

And if they didn't know
Before
What we know
They'll know it
Now

Incontinence

Oh my god—you're leaking!
I can see the dribbles
of blue-black ink scribbling
down your pant leg, pooling
on the floor.   Can you tell?
Can you feel those warm, sticky
words running out of you,
can you see them leaving bright stains
where they've hit the grain?

Maybe you've had too much
to think, and can't contain
it all. Maybe you should have stopped
after that first swallow, if
you can't hold your Jack...
your Ginsberg,
your Baudelaire, or Wordsworth.
Maybe they're too strong for you.

I mean, hard think is not for everyone.

Intoxication can result from just a sip
or two of the strong stuff,
if you aren't used to thinking,
or if it's been too long
since you've indulged.

You could lose control
of your syllables,
might find yourself shacked up
with unfamiliar vocabulary,
might find yourself bursting
with liquid
whizz-key
possibilities
and unable to stop the flow,
once it's begun.

NetWork

Wishes you a HAPPY NEW YEAR! And not just for today, but for all 365 days! Has been out gallivanting today, and now has no gallivant left in her. OOOOOO wwwrrrrrrrrrrrooooooooooHHHHHHHH! Sorry, just felt like howling. Is contemplating the looming spectre of double nickels with a wicked grin. Is feeling groovy. Thinks the snowflakes look like tears. Has made another successful orbit around the sun. Her planets and stars are happy. Life is good. Has just turned on her Lava Light—it's lime green. What color is your Lava Light? Wishes. Is happy! Is still happy! Just saw the first bee of the season. Is singing in the sunshine, dancing in the dirt, wallowing in wonderful, and feeling like a flirt! Oh, give me a few minutes, and I'll come up with a better ending. Has temporarily lost the zippity in her doo-da. Is bakin' in the sunshine, plantin' in the mud, pettin' on her doggies, rejoicin' in her blood—it's Monday and I'm NOT at work! Drove home in the darkness of the encroaching storm, beckoned by jagged fingers of light. lawn chairs and music / poets gather at the park / nothing but sunshine. Has gotta go get red. Has tangerine toenails. And tan lines. Has been cooking like pink honey. black river striped with / red and white city lights, starred / with fireworks' spangles. Is mmellllltiiiing. Felt dirty today. But now she feels clean again. Wants to know with all this melting, how come she isn't losing any weight... should be down to a size 5 by now. Has mined crystal, tasted sweet potato bisque, met an Elvis Presley cousin, splashed in Hot Springs, hand fed a buffalo, and stood at the Crossroads. Oh yeah, and sweated her balls off. Is...let me check. Yep, still happy! Husband James said he just "shocked the pool." I asked him if he lowered his swim trunks at it. LOL! Wishes. And is crossing her fingers. Is still wishing. Fingers still crossed. Is happy. Is OMG look at that full moon, will ya! Is heading for the bunker. Is digging the vibes. Is queueing. Is in an "aliens invade the earth" kind of mood. Is going to HOWL tonight. Is replete with poetry. Is really, really, really happy. Merry Christmahanakwanzadan! May your year shine brightly, my friends. Wishes everyone a very sparkly New Year's Eve.

Red Stilettos

It was difficult, he said,
to come up with new metaphors
for red stilettos,

ones that weren't clichéd,
like blood-covered vampire fangs,
daggered hearts, icicles

reflecting neon light,
the bar floor's erubescent shadows.
He knew he shouldn't

shame such in-your-face
sexiness by using faded similes,
worn-out dungarees of

literary laziness, so he
rifled through his closet of images,
painted himself with allegory,

hitched up his pantyhose,
twitched his skirt, and walked, his two
red pencils editing the night.

Kicking It

Alive and kicking—that's the way the saying goes,
anyway. She's always been alive, *duh*, but she's just
getting around to the kicking. Yeah, it's taken her

awhile, but it's better late than never, and besides,
she knows what she wants to kick now, and who,
and she has some idea where to start, and how.

Who would have thought it could be so complicated?
You just put on your shit kickers and kick some shit,
right? But, no. She realizes one has to work up to

these things, one has to consider and deliberate.
It's not enough to merely be breathing; if you want
anything out of life, you have to be prepared to kick

it in the shins and get its attention. You have to plan
on kicking bad habits and hang-ups, you have to
overcome. You have to study just where to place

the kick for ultimate effectiveness, and you must
practice your kick to attain precision and power.
She knows that sometimes, one kick is all you get.

All you need to do is watch *The Karate Kid* to see
that. Yeah, she's ready to kick it now, to have some
kicks; she's more than ready to get a kick out of life.

Two Bottles

—2010, before Yuengling was sold in Ohio

She bought two bottles of wine, some garlic
and an onion, and is ready to be snowed in.
It's the Solstice, after all, the longest night

of the year, and the full moon combined
with the lunar eclipse (occurring this way
for the first time since 1684) make for a

unique opportunity. Two bottles of wine—
red, of course—and some garlic ought to do
the trick. She already had some avocados

and broccoli on hand, and onion added
to the mix should make for a nice salad.
The garlic's for the snow vampires, if

they make their presence known. She
would have bought some beer, too, but
with a particular craving for Yuengling,

has no hopes of getting any before
the storm barrels in. She grins to think
that, although unavailable for sale in the

state of Ohio, delicious Yuengling comes
to Cleveland regularly in her bloodstream.
Pennsylvanians, who vow to guard their

borders to keep their precious beer from
crossing, fail to detect this audacious
smuggling. She doesn't consider herself

a beer snob, exactly; more an epicure
in the barley malt and hops department.
Ah, well, the eclipse is beginning its

bloody fingerprint, the windowsill is
pungent with garlic, the wine is working
its warm magic. She contemplates stowing

the garlic, pulling an extra glass or two
from the cupboard. It's going to be a long
night, and she's relaxing into it, wanting

someone to talk with. Maybe the snow
vampires will come by, drop in, stay awhile.
Maybe this time, they'll drink...wine.

Family Tree

Elvis didn't really help with the decorating,
but he's taking a nap under the Christmas tree.
Auntie Janis must have worn him out

with all that whiskey and incessant conversation—
I saw her punch him in the arm more than once
for emphasis, when she thought his mind

might be drifting. Bonzo eschewed garlanding,
went to help in the kitchen. I heard him
banging pots and pans (guess he couldn't help

himself, tympani are tympani).   Uncle Jimmy
turned up in time to help with the lights,
holding them up and dancing a bump and grind

while crooning "come on baby, light my fire"
to the delight of the grandchildren. Second
Uncle Jimi, his ever-present guitar strung

across his back, hung the star. Maybe he'll
play a new piece for us after dinner; he always
wakes up the neighborhood when he bends

those strings, and god knows we'll all be
somnolent from the tryptophan in the turkey.
Cousin John brought his buddy and flatmate

Stu; the more, the merrier, I always say,
and besides, Stu cracks us up with his wacky
pencil sketches.   John's a whiz at drawing,

too; they're both so darn talented.   Grandpa
Jerry's in the back room, trying on his Santa suit;
Grandmama Cass had to take it in some

after he lost weight last year. We'll all take
turns sitting on his lap—yes, even the adults—
and have our pictures taken with him

on Christmas morning, while the family
gathers 'round and harmonizes on carols.
It's tradition. Grandmama's got some lungs

on her, I'll tell you—she can belt out lyrics
like nobody's business. Stevie Ray, who
surprised us by dropping in (we didn't think

he'd make it this year), says he has a new
song for us to try, something bluesy. I love
his Texas twang. Oops, looks like Elvis

is waking from his snooze. Ha, ha!
We wrapped a ribbon with a bow around his
neck, and tied tinsel to his blue suede shoes!

Flower Power

—for James

It's nasturtium
this evening, chili
with drizzling rain,
not the kind of weather
you're mint to enjoy
but to endure.
Here we go, taking
thyme to beet
the routine, to sloe down
and aloe ourselves
a night out; we can
dill with the dampness.
I mean, you have to draw
the lime between work
and play at some point.
We've bean busy,
and you can't curry on
without some kind
of break if you carrot all
about your sanity.
Lettuce fennel our
exhaustion into attitude,
pepper our lives with art
and entertainment.
Lettuce go forth and
find some fun...
something will turnip,
I'm certain!
I lovage you.
These are the best daisies
of our lives...
you'd better bay leaf it.

One Peachy Day

smear the white juice
of crushed sunlight
over my breasts
the delirious milk of
summershine
go on tell the sky to
lick me to death
with his hot tongue
of blue music
show him how
to pound out the beat
in my mad blood

all I want is
to sweat topless
under the true language
of skin
legs waxed and lathered

cooking like
pink honey

Cravings

I want to braid hair.
I want to quilt.
I want to be the one
who picks up all the pieces
and glues them back together
when the milk has spilt.
I want to be the ringmaster.
I want to be the chair.
I want to be the FEMA
lion, arriving in a timely
fashion to show the disaster
I care.

No, don't want to be the tsunami,
don't want to be the storm,
don't want to scud through cities
dispersing waves of hysteria
as killer bees would do, but,
oh, I would like to swarm.

I want to be the bristles,
I want to be the paint.
I ache to make life
my canvas; fleck, daub,
stipple my way to masterpiece.
I want to be my own saint.
I want to bark at the neighbors;
I want to disturb the peace.
I want to knock down the fences,
run free in the streets.

I want to be the loaves,
I want to be the fishes.
I want to be the fireflies,
the shooting stars, the candles
on the cake; hell,
I want to be the wishes.
I want to capture this moment

in an amber drop of Kodak
memory and flash
it 'round the world for all to see,
spreading peace and love
and equality and acceptance
and serenity and truth
with contagious passion.

I want to start a revolution,
but without nuclear war.
I want to hack the system,
take decisions about taxes,
education, spending, healthcare,
marriage, and armament
out a whole new door.

I want to be the composition.
I want to be the twist and shout.
I want to Dead Head a tarantella
of hope around the room,
I want to work it all out.
I want to be the fermentation;
I want to be the hops.
I want to intoxicate the nation,
douse everyone in optimism,
pull out all the stops.

I crave to be a part,
the very heart, of this thing
called Change
that everyone's been
raving about.

One Small Step

Hubble's on YouTube
tele-scope it out
it's a step-inside invitation
a belly up to the Milky Way bar
and order a draft
of whatever's on celestial tap
a blast from the past
through honeycombed glass
it's a raucous carnival night
our blue and green bubble
afloat on the fairway
lost in the crowd
just a cell on the skin
of a universe too vast
to comprehend

nebula and quasar
tibia and fibula
somehow all connected
we are here, you are there
yet how can we be anywhere
without being aware
we're but one microscopic dot
on the blotter of the entire universe?
hearse comes to take us and we're gone
while the anything but black
whole of the universe lives on
our backwater galaxy
just a vanity
an affectation you can barely see
with the naked eye

radius and ulna
orbit and circumference
I don't know if you can say
we belong to the universe
or it belongs to us
all our little fuss and bother

hunger and whoring for war
doesn't affect the galaxies
one way or the other
trapezium and trapezoid
trapeze and trampoline
cluster and infrared dust
this spangled event continues
night after night
all those uncurling fists
flinging wide
their confetti
of polychromatic light

we like to think we're inquirers
explorers
"Indiana Jones." Amelia Earhart
setting new records
charting unknowns
we like to feel we're
Asimov, Hawking, Carl Sagan
mindsurfing the Cosmos
mapping the night
unraveling Einsteinian mysteries
of this ring or that moon
or some other sparkly satellite
we like to dream
we're lifting the lid
of a sleepy god's eye
and peering inside
we like to imagine
that we can see
behind the curtain
that we have star sight

but here we are
unmasked and marked as rubes
not so much Magellan
as Mr. Magoo
bumbling around our little system
blinded and blistered

by a golden solar spotlight
waving our umbrellas
like swords at the reign
of destruction and hate
not even noticed as gatecrashing ants
under the Big Top of the Bang
all but invisible
wistful and wishful
our bubble world
an impermanent shimmer
ready to pop
at the drop of The Bomb

Hubble's on YouTube
there for the asking
a blast from the past
irising open and inviting us in
one small step and we're through
the metaphysical door
one small step and we've gone
where no one has gone before
and if we go exploring
we just might discover
that we're already there
might discover ourselves
in the stardust
of what's already here
(and whether or not
we find any Others
or they find us)
we aren't lost
to this Universal history

our tickets are punched
and we're *all* of us
along for the trip
on this mindblowing
cosmic
Möbius strip

Black and White

let love go for good
and make the night your sanctuary

how could we believe in something
so full of the glow of day

when these dark shadows
are fecund with the breath of peace

it's time to hide here
in this quiet world

where our names are secret
and no one can follow

protected by a moon so ripe
it must be about to burst

Cary Grant Walks

Cary Grant (1904-1986)

along the beach
discarded cigarette
still glowing

copper penny sun
slips beneath the waves
gilding bare ankles

melting into shadow
hands in his pockets
counting the stars

Frank Sinatra Sighs

Frank Sinatra (1915-1998)

as neon pales
into the light of dawn
another goodbye

through the doorway
a spill of sunshine
his empty bottle

out of sight
his song carries back
on the wind

Soul Custody*

Arthur Lee (1945-2006)

an angel traced your copper face
another kissed your throat
with one hand warm
behind your neck
another pulled you close

they held their breath
and cupped their ears
your songs unsilenced by your death
they wept away
your wasted years
and took you into custody
the angels have you, Arthur Lee

you set the scene at center stage
and then refused to play
the game was done
the world moved on
and Love was fade-away

you whispered to the gods and gave
your soul *and more again*
for music's sake
the angels smiled
¡que vida! está bien

they held their breath
and cupped their ears
your songs unsilenced by your death
they wept away
your wasted years
and took you into custody
the angels have you, Arthur Lee

incorporates song titles by Arthur Lee / Love

Serious Moonlight

David Bowie (1947-2016)

"Life is but a dream..."—William Shakespeare

Rising from a swimmer's dream
of coral and dappled light, he skims
off the beads of sleep that slick his
eggshell skin. The sky turns to smoke.
Night is serious here, where shadows
bend silver to their will. The round
nipple of the full moon rises....

We taste the blood of his music,
hold it on our tongues and remember
vanished flowers

Trick Whore Treat

he tricks me out, treats me
like I'm a prostitute
he's paying for the privilege
of abusing, using me
as an emotional shunt
a sick excuse for his messy
fucked up confessional blues
schmoozing me
into the metaphorical sack
while stabbing me
in the back—hell, in the front
in a typically
egotistical testicular attack

is it something I lack?
does he think I'm weak?
he doesn't speak to the others
in the room—all men—the same
way, as if coming from the womb
with feminine mystique
is a mistake
of a meek Mother Nature
making him naturally superior
giving him stature
putting me out to pasture
well let me blunt
he's wrong about one thing—

he's the cunt

Merrily, Merrily

Life is
but a dream
a scream
a supremely
funny joke
being played
on us by a sick
universe
a masquerade
paraded
by a god
who likes to poke
dead things
with a stick

Life is
but a dream
ice cream
melting
in a beam
of sunlit madness
more or less
a mess
I guess
we know
the score, poor
fools that we are
ROTFLOL
as we all
float on down
the stream...

Easter/West

Wood Jesus
Wok upon water
Wood he
Skip metaphysical
Stones
Break metaphorical
Bones
Stir the base
Ingredients
And come out on top?

Wood Jesus
Rise like dough
Wood he
Knead the bread
Of life
And watch it grow
Bake it
Break it
Taste it
And let go?

Wood Jesus
Wine about his
Blood
Wood he
Dine one last time
With his brood
Water
Down the mood
Turn it into
Something good?

Wood Jesus
Be cross
If he knew the score
Wood he
Rock the foundations

Of the world
Stone us
Into submission
With his admission
Of un/holy war?

Baby Needs a New Pair of Wings

What thumbprint
sealed my fate, consigned me
to this place, to be a joke
among such happy souls?
The fools around me roll
the die, barter for another try:

C'mon, c'mon, c'mon
Baby needs a new pair of wings
Snake Eyessss

I ache to grapple with the odds,
wrestle with the croupier,
scale the heights, make my
escape from all these broken
seraphim and their fallen God.

I want to love and be loved
in return. I want to burn
with all the passions of a life
well justified, not with
regrets. I want to win.

But, no. The game is Craps
and Snake Eyes come up
every time. There's no
chance here; the fix is in.
I'm trapped in God's amusement
park of Hell. His Snake Eyes
narrow. Forget the sparrow; His
eye is on the prize
of viper's sting. The fools roll die;
oblivious to their demise.

C'mon, c'mon, c'mon...
Baby needs
a new pair of wings

Night Ballet

He is black ice,
a dark poison smear.

Her car hits him,
and dances the road
in frantic circles.

Why would a woman drive
to her death
on night's concrete?
Why would she slow down
to listen to the wild growl
of winter wind,
and be made foolish
by its whisper?

How could she do it,
knowing one slip
on that raw skin of glass
could rip her heart,
drain her blood,
and bring out her sad ghost?

She is so bare of color
that she is but a shadow,
squirming for air.

All the salt of God and oceans
will not melt her free.

Black Mass

The trees are dark,
and the spaces
between them
are filled with
arcane murmurings:
barbed-wire
confessions
and sweet-lipped
communions,
promising change.

The trees are dark,
and bruise
the earth
with their fisted
shadows.
They clench
the soft folds
of her skin
in their talons;
they eat
of her flesh
and grow strong.

The trees are dark,
and lacerate
the sky.
They lift
thorny chalices
to collect
the tears
of heaven;
they drink the stars.

The trees are dark,
and their slow dance
dresses the altar,
brings the black

candles to flame.
And their breath
is the incense
of musk, and of myrrh.

The trees are dark.

You may call One,
if you know its Name.

Purdah

in the crucible
of their relationship
he beat her
soft porcelain body
into a gray powder
mixed it
with the ashes
of her tears
and swallowed
her whole

the newspaper
did not remark upon
her hair the color
of mud
nor the child
curled like a fist
inside her womb

Daisy Chain

The rape
of flowers in their beds.
Triumphant buzz
of the pillagers;
bulk, suffocation,
silken heads convulsing.
A torrent
of new history.
Involuntary regurgitation
of seed
to air redolent
of bruised blossoms
and muddy decay.
Their pale faces turned
blindly toward the light;
all those
silent yellow Os
of horror.

Countdown

boom

Blue Heart

in the corner
Frank Sinatra
spills his mood
into the room
moonlight crawls
across the carpet
have another
shot of gloom

in the wee small
hours of morning
lulled by whiskey
mauled by love
smoke rings
disappear
in shadow
anger gives
the heart a shove

keeping vigil
with the nightbred
sleeping now
would be a crime
every blue heart
finds redemption
in the alcohol
of time

All I Want Is to Leave

Tomorrow is a hard luck story, today's
Over before you know it. All I want is to
Leave the blues behind. I'm sick of blue;
Every day, nothing to wear but blue.
All I want is to leave the blues behind.
Veins of cobalt, denim, indigo run deep,
Establish tributaries, steep, stew, delve into and
Thieve my peace of mind. All I want is to be
Happy, realize my potential, find some
Excitement, break some limits. I want to
Buy a new car, take it farther than I've ever been,
Leave the blues in the dust. I want to win,
Unleash the beast of success, make the best of my
Experience; I want to excel, I want to groove.
Screw the blues! All I want is to leave the
Blues behind. I want to turn yesterday around,
Escape its reach. I don't want anything
Handed to me; just give me a chance. All
I want is to leave the blues behind. I want to fly.
Now is the time to wash them out of my hair.
Dammit, Mr. Blue Sky, bye-bye.

Brother, Can You Spare a Dime

The dollar is dolor, downsized
and getting smaller. Although
colorized, lacking color.
Bad, a little mad, and
altogether too serious.
Mysteriously
vanishing,
acting out
its lack
of good
¢

Check Out

If you have a card, please scan it now.

We are reduced to the lowest
common denominator,
assigned a series of digits
zero through nine,
mixed, matched, and entered
(if we're lucky)
online, designed to function as
a thin plastic card, a blip
on the scanner, all our data configured,
refigured, disfigured, defaced, consigned
to a magnetic strip
that's all too easily damaged
or erased.

Yeah, we're asleep, on the nod
from a number fix—
old man Fraud up to his trademart tricks.
Don't pay now! what you can owe later.
Hey, give me some credit
where credit is due;
all hail the revolution, Caesar's god,
and the microchip for coming up
with this red over black (dis)solution.
Lack of funds?
No problem, just send back this handy
application, and we'll add you
to our stacks.

And what about that nasty identity
theft? Not much is left after
your name is crossed out, and you
become just another greased cog
in the massive mazed money machine.
No, it's no fun to find yourself stolen,
rogered up the bum, dropped

in a hole, lost in the cracks,
a runaway train out of control
and hopping the tracks,
headed for disaster,
faster and faster,
card charged to the max.

Truth is, we've been thrown under
the bus, chopped up, popped in
the blender and juiced,
an homogenized economy promised
the moon, dandled, fondled, bread-fed,
and ultimately set loose,
encouraged to (re)produce a fashionable,
irrational debt. We are stamped,
sealed and delivered,
basket cases
left on the banker's doorstep,
castaways fated to lose
this thankless, luckless lottery
of financial strife.

It all adds up to exactly
nothing. We have become plastic
Frankensteins bereft of life,
faceless antiheroes.
We have become all ones.
We have become all zeros.

*If you are finished scanning, please
press finish and pay*

now.

Few Dollar Man

my Cleveland, I don't mind him
being a blue collar, few dollar man

don't need him all prettified,
gentrified, riverwalked,
starched, pressed and lean
I like his urban sprawl
his sports bars,
sports cars,
Ford trucks,
Great Lakes brew and bratwurst,
his rib fests and bare chests

he can put on a suit and tie
if the occasion calls for it
he cleans up real nice
he's no "playhouse square"
he's a comfortable fit

I like his long hair, level stare,
acting like he doesn't care,
blue jean and boots swagger,
his never-say-die attitude,
his rock and roll hammer
I dig the pensive, ponytailed,
punkass poet in him

I like it when he shows his
ethnic roots

and I don't mind his often gruff speech,
his questionable grammar
don't mind his broken English,
city slang or down-home twang,
his sometimes breach
of political tact
and cultural fact
we have an understanding

I don't mind his tough sidewalks,
his callused highways,
the clumsy fumble of his
tumbledown neighborhoods
don't mind the times his rough
street lighting catches at my clothes
in the heavy dark
when he's running his transit
through my hair

at least, he's reaching out for me,
wants to feel me close against him

I don't mind the stubble
on his troubled street corners,
cold Lake Erie steaming his breath,
his bleary neon eyes,
his wasted wallpaper billboards
too many nights of revel
after long days spent
in steelwork,
car shops,
west side markets
and east side offices,
orange-barreled highway construction,
Clinic halls
and University malls
working,
giving all he's got,
just making a living

I trust him; I know he has my back,
know he's looking out for me
he's an honest S.O.B.

my Cleveland, I don't mind him
being a blue collar, few dollar man

Cleveland Spelled Backwards Is

DNA
Level C
twisted for sure
helical hysterical
mythical miracle
under and inside my skin
you are what makes me
tick makes my pulse
quicken thickens my blood
and lightens my mood
you are the call of the wild
cinema saint and soul food
for thought soup kitchen broth
scatological lyrical
metaphorical physical
history quizzical
and musically blessed
dressed in the riches
and rags of the past
DNA
Level C
unwinding at last
blinding in beauty
revealing a ceiling
unreachable
mystery teachable
to all of us craning our necks
for a glance
at the molecules dancing
faster and faster
and picking up speed
the hues
of the rainbow a revolution
a legacy amassing a levy
see? we are the fee
and we are the payment
undressing
and raiment

DNA
Level C
yes we are the cost
and we are the catalyst
the movement the go and the flow
and all
that we foment
this spotlighted moment
the past and the future
intrinsic to truth
and remastered by youth
word wizards
spell casters
and pompous bombasters
mystical whimsical
and what does it matter
if we drop the ball
this whole ball of wax
it's the all and the awe of it
twisted for sure
and lost in the stacks
a spiraling virus
that cures as it curses
twisted two fisted thick
wristed red lipped
it nips as it nurses
complicated and sated
outside and inside
it's you
and it's me
D
N
A
L
e
v
e
l
C

Casting Call

Where are the men
who used to rip off their shirts
and brawl outside the bar

beneath a street lamp? Where
are the Stanleys who call for
their Stellas, where

are the barrel-chested Mitchums
who speak in the man-code
of heavy-lidded eyes,

deep breaths taken and held
hostage in silences?
Where are the Roger

O. Thornhills, resourceful
and elegant, suited and hatted
and taking the train,

the Humphrey Bogarts giving
it all up for love and Paris,
the Jimmy Cagneys resplendent

in rolled-up shirt sleeves
and slaps on the back and hey
Mac, hey Buddy, got a light

bonhomie? Where are
the Bonds who wink and seduce
with glass-clinking diplomacy,

Mephistophelian wisdom,
irresistible threat? Where
are the Richard Burtons

never at a loss for words,
raising hell along with their
silver-tongued toasts?

And where is that cache
of cool women swathed
in pearls, sheathed in glittering,

floor-length sophistication?
Where are the Ilsas, the Eves,
soft-voiced and resolute,

unfaltering in sagacity
and poise? Where are
the sultry Sophias pouting

and purring for ardor;
the Avas, whose vixen red
lips never smear?

Where are the doe-eyed
Bacalls who know how
to whistle, steadfast

and sure in hurricanes
and gun battles and affairs
of the heart? Where are

the Alva Starrs, the Daisy
Clovers, unripened
and vulnerable, crammed with

ambition, chewing adversity;
where are the Liz Taylors,
born knowing how to drive

frangible stakes into permafrost
with their lavender scrutiny?
And where, where

are the valiant Stellas
who interpret their ruggedly
flawed Stanleys, who burn

through the roles they play,
where are the Stellas who never
flinch, who never think twice

about all those bars or the brawling
under street lamps...Stellas
evolving, Stellas, triumphant?

Happy Hour

—Bar Louie, Crocker Park, 2013, with James, Geri, and John

She had a "Kiss my Aztec,"
I had an "Effen Good"—

not so much a Hemingway
as a Burroughs moment.

That Beat Generation knew
how to party. It might be

all rum and umbrellas in
Cuba and the Florida Keys,

but Cleveland winter calls for
cool cucumber and the splash

of icy mint, an indecently
naked lunch of tequila,

chocolate, and coffee liqueur,
cocktails that scream

from the soft machine of
an indifferent bartender's hands.

Got Soul?

—after graffiti on a brick wall, Artomatic 419, Toledo, OH

Cities have souls too, you know,
some malignant and ugly,
sneering, full of derision;
some benign and beautiful,
some merely indifferent
and uninviting, bland, lacking
ambiance, pizzazz, character.

Some cities spit dust.
Some cities swallow without chewing first.
Some cities rust out before their time,
arthritic and osteoporotic,
empty windows, crumbling bricks,
wasted motion.
Some cities are pitiful, joints aching
with unfulfilled dreams.
Some cities are pugilistic,
insolent, provocative,
legs apart, arms akimbo,
daring you to knock the chips off
their blocks, ready to solve their problems
with fists and amplified voices.
Some cities squander their chances
in one gamble too many.
Some cities have had it up to here.

Some cities blush with cheeks
of blooming fruit trees, invite you in
for tea and an afternoon of discussing
the latest New York Times best seller,
genteel with old money.
Some cities are steepled and mapled,
recycle and go green and please don't litter.
Some cities lick their lips and turn on
the red light and say baby, baby, don't be
afraid, it's only money and you're not a cop,

are you?

Some cities say everything's for sale.
Some cities say you can't touch this.
Some cities wear their rainbows with pride.

Some cities are limos and taxies
and underground trains.
Some cities bicycle to lunches of wraps
and salads and unsweetened tea.
Some cities take their coffee black.
Some cities drink only bottled water.
Some cities hunker down and slurp
right from the river.

Some cities are lazy, dingy,
busted streetlights, broken bottles,
peeling billboards, gutter trash.
Some cities sleep on the streets
and wheedle spare change.
Some cities are caricatures of themselves.
Some cities feel like prison walls.

Some cities offer you a light,
a couch for the night, a bowl of soup,
the shirts off their backs.
Some cities sing in unfamiliar voices,
move in alien rhythms, but beg you
to join in anyway.

Some cities coruscate in sunlight, effervescent
with laughter and confident of time.
Some cities glow soft in the darkness, like
fireflies seen from a rooftop, neoned
and open all night.
Some cities close their eyes and pretend
you're not even there.
Some cities are come-as-you-are,
let it all hang out, let's hold hands and
put a flower in the government's rifle.

Some cities cry over spilled milk.
Some cities look the other way.

These are not my city.

My city is hardscrabble.
My city is plodding and stodgy
and weighed down by the grime on its neck
and the dirt under its fingernails.
My city works hard for the money, blue collared,
blue jeaned, blues on the radio, rock in its roll,
tired to its soul
but dragging out of bed in the morning
for one day closer to retirement.
My city has dogs in the backyard,
motorcycles in the garage;
my city cashes its checks
and goes to the movies,
bets on the Lottery,
reads poetry when nobody's watching.
My city cheers for the underdog.

My city has Great Lakes in the refrigerator
and Wonder Roast on the table.
My city just opened fresh bags of chips
and Cheetos, my city is pulling up
an extra chair.
My city is holding the door open.
My city slaps you on the back,
offers you a brew, says
come on in, willya, and wipe your feet, and
welcome to the neighborhood.

Thaumaturgy

walking on water
that's not so tough
all you have to do is imagine
that you are as light as air
and as insubstantial
as an unexpressed thought

all you have to do
is look down at the wrinkled bed
of glistening water
and move one foot in front
of the other
balancing on the trampoline
of waves

all you *have* to do is ignore
the catcalls of those
who tell you it's impossible
against the laws of nature
their voices faint
as you walk farther
and farther
and farther
from the shore

Frankie's Too Cool

—after Francis Albert Sinatra

Frankie, he's too cool to be depressed.
I mean, look at the way this cat is dressed:
jacket, hanky, shirt and tie, his trousers pressed,
his hat set back on his head, and one of the songs
he's best known for on his lips and in his throat.
He's singing like there's no tomorrow; even if his
voice does convey sorrow, his eyes betray the lies
his lyricist wrote, because you and I both know
he just borrows the feeling, puts on a show, steals
our emotions, gets us to follow along and identify
with somebody else's matrimonial mess.

It's ok, man, Frankie's too cool to be depressed.
He doesn't need sleep like the rest of us; he's
blessed with unlimited drive. That cat's alive!
You know? Wherever he goes, the party starts
when he arrives. He keeps the joint jumping,
keeps his joint humping, keeps the blood
pumping, plays his part to perfection. He's a
twenty-four-hour incorrigible erection, jump-
jiving and wailing, nailing the chicks and swinging
the dicks, mixing his music with the sweet
by and by of just sitting and sipping his Jack,
stacking the hours like poker chips, flipping
a c-note for a ten percent tip.

Man, Frankie's *way* too cool to be depressed.
He might get mad; can't blame a brother for that,
but he's kicking sad in the nuts, knocking the blues
back on their butts, shaking fists, making faces,
and shooting the finger to all the naysayers
and players who would drag him down. Man,
he *owns* this town! He's kissing yesterday's ass
goodbye. He doesn't truck with depression,
and from now on, I'm not messing around; I'm
taking my lessons from him. You don't tell me

I can't—I *can*. I'm gonna give it all, all I have to give.
I'm too cool to be depressed. Man, from now on,

I'm gonna *live*.

Bohemian Vendetta

blue warrior
pursuing your bohemian
vendetta against
the unrealized dreams
of nothing
is ever what it seems
to be
clutching in your
karmic arms
the fractured promises
of your mistaken identity
and you were so sure
you had found yourself
this time

Going Braless

She spent too many decades defined by edges—
now, she's taking a metaphorical bath, soaking,

melting away the corners, feeling all fuzzy
and edgeless. She imagines losing the edges

in her life is a lot like going braless:
there's that dizzying snap of freedom, gravity

tugging at the sudden softness, the tingle
of unexpected stimuli, the shift in physical

awareness. There's the feeling of breaking
with what's expected of her, breaking habits,

the exhilaration of defying convention,
embracing informality, thumbing her nose

at the status quo. No more edges! She's done
with angles, borders, bulwarks.

From now on, she'll be all curves and arches,
graceful loops, swooping curls, calligraphy.

Conscientious Objector

Don't want to be put in a you-niform.
Don't want to be marshalled into you-nity.
Don't want to be assimilated into
the rank and file,
marched along smartly,
don't want to be dog-tagged and ten-miled.
Don't want to be ordered and orderly,
don't want the corners
of my blanket tucked,
bed made up tight as a drumhead.
Don't want to be boxed in,
forced to fit, all straight line
and eyes forward,
pushed up and put down,
No rattatattat for me.

My music billows.
It waltzes and tarantellas
like a dervish in psychedelic estrus,
it harpsichords and theremins
in unearthly scales.
My music rolls on the floor
with impossible abandon,
hangs inverted from the pole,
defies gravity,
does wild splits,
gets down and dirty.
My music jumps
way out of line, gives authority
the finger, swears in another language.

My music won't be quarantined.
It ripples and radiates
like a fifty-five kiloton atomic
virus, flashes
flowerchild peace signs
in all directions.
It positions daisies in the bore holes

94

of rifles, drapes love beads
on strands of razor wire,
backpacks into the wilderness
wearing only a smile.
It uncages the animals.
It smears lipstick
on your collar.
My music says no
as much as it says yes.

I don't want to be put into a you-niform.
I don't want to be marshalled into you-nity.
The general idea is this, man:
I don't want to be all I can be.
I want to be all I *am*.

Serious Flannel

Ten degrees outside
and though much warmer
inside, she's breaking out
the *serious* flannel tonight.

None of that silly flannel,
the pinched and scrawny
kind, the kind that minces
about afraid to commit to

what it was made for, not
for her. None of that thin
and pretend flannel,
delusional and deluding,

aiming for fashion, trying
to make a statement,
none of those skinny bolls
of cotton, nor polyester

balls, neither. No sir, she
wants the *serious* flannel,
the real thing. She wants
thick, deliberate, substantial,

ample cotton cocooning
her, she wants flannel that
flaunts its purpose, fluffy,
furry, fat and fabulous,

flannel that knows what
it's for, flannel that doesn't
care what you think, flannel
that's *out* of the closet.

Cupid

Cupid at long last is dead
I shot that bastard in the head
you'll find him lying in the street
crumpled wings and dirty feet
one less misery to mourn
one less day of his deceit
now I'm free to be reborn
now I'm free to be complete
don't need that fucker in my bed
Cupid at long last is dead

Her First Time

Casting aside all doubt
and giving in to wild abandon,
she strips off her clothes
and steps into the delicious swirl
of hot tub,
sinks into the wet fever
of water's kiss...

thick steam
rising like incense
toward heaven

Story Book
—a poem for two voices, to be read simultaneously
Hers   His

Hers	His
Me,	Me,
you,	you,
dawn,	dawn,
sheets twisted	and a damp bed
and your thin wrists	rumpled by our romp
and delicate feet	last night.
intoxicating	I don't remember
my senses far more	all of it; I guess
than this empty bottle	this empty bottle
could ever do. There is	accounts for that lapse.
only you in all this world.	What I do recall was great;
I don't care about ever after;	you really had me going!
All I care about is right now.	Thank god you didn't whine
All I care about is	on about commitment,
one more time	happy ever-
with you.	after,
Us.	"us."

Psalm

let me
lick
your toffee skin
as warm
as intoxicating
as buttered rum
your eyes
a temple
your lips
both honey
and sting

let me
stroke
your sunflower
shoulders
tease
sweet nectar
from your
swollen nipples
my thighs
tickled
by your thorn

let me
whisper
silk and smoke
into the coral
blush of
your ears
let me
catch
your starry seed
in the soft
indigo sweater
of my
night

In This Desert

soft
snakeskin blur
of night
drawn by
the heat
of your
body

nestled
in the hollows
sharing
your sleep
coiling
next to you
begging
your breath

flickering
taste of
your
sex

Each Stroke a Promise

his pale body
was the page
upon which she wrote
the calligraphy
of her passion

graceful loops
and swooping curls
enigmatic exclamation points
her tongue pressed
against his eyelids

her fingertips boldly
staining his chest
a brush of ink at his groin
whispering her manuscript

each stroke a promise

Wood I Love You

there's all kinds of wood
hard, soft, whatever you want
I like naughty pine

Summer and Smoke

he holds his cock
like a paintbrush
touches her
white body
with long
careful strokes
he trails magenta
flame down
her spine
feathering
the edges
he dips
again and again
into the bright wet
pools of color
finishes
with stipples
of sweat
and cum

sometimes late
at night and alone
she dreams
the blush
of the rising sun

and she can hear
his Picasso
and she can taste
his Monet

Making Scents

the smell of you

the coming closer tell of you
the ringing bell of you
the welcomed sight and relished bite
and every electric honeyed cell of you
the tart anise pizzelle of you
the sweet caramel of you

the artesian well of you
the pell-mell, unparalleled mind of you
the mellowed, gentle kind of you
the stellar, *mach schnell* drive of you
the shrapnelled, unquelled life of you
the velvet knife of you

the give 'em hell of you
the rebel yell and shotgun shell
and black magic spell of you

the a capella song of you
the fella I belong to you
the way you make my legs go jello you
the helter-skelter, gimme shelter
summer swelter, I'll stop the world and melt
with you
the hotel, motel, no-tell bed of you
the nobel prize in size of you
the swell of you

the smell of you

Sugar Spice and Everything Twice

the taste of you

the making my heart race of you
the making my heart ache for you
the let's make haste
don't wanna wait of you
the wrap my legs around your waist
of you
the rattle roll and shake of you
the moving heaven and earth-
quake of you

the salt and sweet and spicy hot of you
the what the heck why not of you
the naughty wicked wit of you
the slender fingered fit of you
the wet my pussy spit of you
the never will say quit of you

the baby you're so street of you
the no one can compete with you
the you make me complete of you
the teasing pleasing tongue of you
the heat of your lust treat of you
the ooh you get so hard of you
the you make me see stars of you
the pluck the strings of my guitar of you
the lick my mind and suck my diction
sense of humor, fact and fiction
of you

the coffeed breath and grind of you
the simple and complex of you
the age-, sex-, color-blind of you
the all wound up and then unwind of you
this moment frozen

     here

in time with you
the kisses quick and stroking slow of you
the privacy and show of you
the I will never know
enough of you
the lips, the hair, and eyes of you
the rise to heaven fall to hell of you

the sight the touch the sound the smell
of you

the taste of you

You Are You

You
are soulful, full of jazz
devil-may-care and devil-may-stare
sassy, smart assy and buyer beware
popcicle sweet and lollipop treat
lickable, sweat-stickable
teaseable and pleasable
You

are
the blues, smoking hot
stirring the pot and not just to look at
but touchable. Sexy? So muchable
you are the cream of the crop
the cream in my coffee, steamy,
dreamy and good to the last drop
You

are
the rock in my roll, the tick in my clock
a fusion of music, tranceable, danceable,
street and hip-hop, second glanceable
yesterday's feature, tomorrow's top
news and the presses don't
stop
You

are
the when of my future
the who in my present,
the why of my past
the where of my heartbeats
the answer to everything I've ever
asked
You

Butterfly

When we
are in the middle
of making love
and you are on top
of me
thrusting away
inside me

your dark eyes
unfathomable
swallowing me

my captive heart
fluttering helplessly
pinned
like butterfly wings
to this mattress of passion

you hook
my thigh
in the crook of your
pale arm

and open me like
a rosebud
my petals
spread wider
for you

my heart
fluttering
surrenders
to the net
of your lust

drowns
in the killing jar
of your silent cry

These Places

sound like some astronomer's
wet dream

labia majora
clitoris
gluteus maximus
areola

sensations launched
from fingerpads
streaking from
point to point
traveling at the speed
of a synaptic kiss

this astronaut blinded
by the constellations
forming in your sweat-slick
pale universe

looking for that
Big Bang

Wet

Shell I tell you
how I feel?

I sea you
in my dreams,
and a wave
of craving
inundates me.
I splash
skinnydip
in the sensations
of your smile,
I am caught
in the net
of your eyes.

I'm shore
this love
will not leave
with the tide.

You anchor
my heart
with yours,
oar,
shell I say,
you swim
in my blood.

Am I naughtycal
for admitting...

you
make me
wet

Pink Hell

the other day
I read
where someone had written
that hell
was not black and hot
after all
(you know
all vast and vaporous
brimstone
and lake-of-fire)
but pink and wet

and I'm not sure
how they knew that
but it made sense to me

I can see hell being all
squishy and squirmy
and uncomfortably moist
worm-ridden
and dank-smelling
like the worst basement
you've ever been in

its floor yielding
to your footsteps
like slippery mud
only it's not mud
but blood
or mucus
or some other
pink-tinged
viscous
body fluid
with its puckered walls
closing in
swelling about you
like the muscles

112

of a uterus
around a fetus

and I can see where
you could find yourself
unable to back out
once you've entered in
feeling all
panicky
trapped
and claustrophobic

and you can't catch
your breath
and you can't see
an inch before you
only that damned
gelatinous
pinkness
and you're engulfed

and you know
it's too late now
nothing is ever born
again here

Bufo Alvarius*

poor complexion
spotted, warty, squat
the color of bile

Bufo alvarius
psychedelic
sin-sweet sweat
produces
amphibian hallucination

toke a toad today

jump out of your skin
into his
and back again

illegal substance
but what the heck
we're all gonna croak
someday

*The venom secreted by this toad can be dried into the illegal drug bufotenine and smoked to create a high stronger than created by the psychedelic properties of LSD.

Dark Shadow

Jonathan Frid (1924-2012)
—r.i.p. Barnabas Collins

Shadow of what I once was,
a gray and fleeting child of night,
I pass and fade like winter rain.

I lost a love that cost my life
and lost the warmth that most derive
from pulsing blood in heart and vein.

I shun the sun, that mocking light
that fails to touch me, as it does
the world of living, with its fire,

for I am chilled in flesh and bone
since losing passion from my own
life, tortured now by bitter bane.

And what if I were mad, insane?
Release! If it were only known
how sad it is to be alone.

Living dead, with no desire
for life, but losing choice since I
forfeited death for memory.

For loving overmuch, my crime,
I now atone by wandering on
to seek another like that one.

So, do not fear the twilight's time;
that fading rustle is but me,
a sad, dark shadow, passing by...

The Nightmare Spinners

last night
you saw
the angels die
their wings
dragged fire
across the sky
there's no escape
when spinners fly
hush child
it won't help
to cry

and when the gates
of heaven fell
the ashes
spiraled down
the well
to pool
in craters
black as hell
hush child
I've some more
to tell

let guilty
pleasures
be your guide
for on their backs
the nightmares
ride
like frightened sheep
the hours hide
hush child
let us
come inside

you claim
you're not impressed
by sin
but let the show
of hands begin
don't you know
we'll always win
hush child
we're
already
in

Wraiths

Paper-thin, these words
between us;
gauzy, and without marrow.

We can see right through them,
and they were never meant

to carry weight.
They tease
us, play with our eyes,
curtains blowing
ghostlike
in the wind.

They don't last long.

They never touch the skin.

Fusion

Molten steel, these words
between us;
brazen, and without pretense.

We can't hold onto them,
for they are far too heavy

for either of us alone.
They mock
us, play with our eyes,
hot coals glowing
demonical
in oil and sin.

They will last for always.

They brand, they melt
themselves into our skin.

Learning the Form

—haiku by John Burroughs

Longer I live, more I learn
Efficiency, economy, paring down of
All speech into small packages,
Rounding out sentences into slim lines,
Not wasting what little I have.
I wrote this haiku one
Night, while waiting for sleep:

Grab your dusty hat,
Throw it in the fire with mine.
Have to let brains breathe.

Easy to do, if you have the proper
Form in your mind: use
Only what you need, discard the
Rest, and make sure what's left
Makes some kind of sense.

Mutability

—by John Burroughs
—*by Dianne Borsenik*

She asked me for lines
to begin her new renku.
I Googled the word.

His coffee mug empty, he
sips at the font of knowledge.

He asked her to change
the first person in his third
line to third: I, he.

Wisteria sways
in the breeze. Even oaks move
with persistent wind.

He'll serve no lines before their
time, no matter how she whines.

Six months, six stanzas—
bowing to oak's obstinance,
renku is rengay.

Jawbone

—Kent, Ohio, the 1st weekend in May

She wagged her jawbone
for three days straight, spitting

and spewing words right
and left, circling the city

like a Hinckley buzzard
coming home to roost,

but her wings were stanzas
and her swoops, rhyme,

and there was nothing but
life everywhere she looked.

She wagged her jawbone
for three days straight, splitting

her infinitives and dangling
her participles, all in the name

of poetic festival, sounds
waltzing on tympanic

membranes, a moveable
feast of words all the

hues of time, tattooed
on sidewalks of skin.

She wagged her jawbone
for three days straight, fitting

square into round and round
into hexagonal, a strange

magic of acceptance and trust,
the warm night opening her

like a dandelion spore,
lifting her, carrying her

farther and farther into the
soft fur of a black squirrel sky.

Communication Breakdown

this fiction in my dictionary
is frictional and so contrary
never dull, nor ordinary
but sensational, and scary

language is a lie
communication zombiefied
splatter movie effects

a gory story of tortured plot
rotting clots of consonants and vowels
disemboweled by sickles and scythes
metaphorical and metaphysical
sibilants and gutturals
left on the ground
howling fricatives and plosives
allegorical and quizzical
giblets and offal
wet gobbets of sound

artificially superficial
facially spatial
temporary and transitory
wickedly wasteful

improvisationally scripted
stripped from maxilla's muscle
mandible's tongue
bitten from palate
enamel and lung
snorted from sinuses
snotty in tone
distorted inflection
forced through the bone

desperate air
rushing to suicide
against concrete/perception

weals of meaning clean and obscene
(don't know what you mean)
dissolved in the acids
of syntax and accent
(can't tell what you meant)
an accident waiting to happen
merely a hint

language is a grand illusion
communication breakdown
all blister and bluster and ooze

clusters of gruesome, noisome refuse
doomed to die the minute they fly

the dick-shun in my dick-shunary
is sick and scabrous, leprous, hairy
dribbling syllables, inflammable
burning like the dickens, blamable

a latex cicatrix
the actor wears
a mask
unasked
a second skin
lubricated with the ichor
of limitation and decay
disguising the true smooth
unbroken, unspoken
body
of what I'm really
dying to say.

Mother Tongue

my mother tongue
is not English
does not consist of dialect
nor regional accent
cannot be confined
by borders
fences, gates, oceans
or mountain ranges
cannot be defined
by fricatives or plosives
sibilants or gutturals
does not dwell in
maxilla or mandible
palate, enamel,
lip, or lung,
cannot be carried on air
nor discerned by ear
cannot be interpreted
by the speech-pattern area
of the human brain

you will not find
my mother tongue
in a dictionary
thesaurus, newspaper,
nor encyclopedic codex
my mother tongue
has never
appeared in public
wearing any form
of covering

my mother tongue
antecedes civilization
is older than spoken
alphabets
does not recognize
nouns or verbs

adverbs, adjectives,
prepositions, interjections
or conjunctions
my mother tongue
rejects politics
rejects religion
rejects delineation
and rejects punctuation

my mother tongue
does not obey orders
does not genuflect
does not curtsey
has never sworn
fealty to kings, queens,
shahs, imams, emperors,
prime ministers, presidents,
popes, czars, rajahs or gurus
my mother tongue
will not kiss your ring
my mother tongue
has never been conquered
or contained

you cannot destroy
my mother tongue
with atomic weapons
or other weapons of
mass destruction
you cannot slash it with
machetes, nor shock it
with tasers
you cannot shoot it
with cannons or missiles
or lasers or guns
my mother tongue
will spit out your bullets
with a grin

drugs have no effect on

my mother tongue
they do not blunt
or numb
or paralyze it
do not elicit
blurred murmurings
from it
my mother tongue
never loses control
my mother tongue
can drink you
under the table

my mother tongue
does not get snowed in
or plowed under
does not wither
does not turn brittle
does not go to seed
my mother tongue
lives off the land
my mother tongue
knows which way
the wind blows

my mother tongue
will tickle your fancy
Monet your name
at the crest of orgasm
boldly Van Gogh where
no tongue has gone before
my mother tongue
says "*An-Dalí, arriba!*"
my mother tongue
says "*Picasso, su casa*"

my mother tongue
is not Haydn
in the shadows
it promises "I'll be Bach"

my mother tongue
can Handel the pressure
my mother tongue
swiveled with Presley
flounced with Liberace
gyrated with Jackson
took wing with Nureyev
and danced dirty with Swayze
my mother tongue
is the cat's meow

my mother tongue
denies domestication
and refuses extinction
my mother tongue
salaams epiphany
namastes the inevitable
daps possibility
my mother tongue
kisses both cheeks
of experience
my mother tongue
vibrates
on a perfect note
in infinite sustain

my mother tongue
crosses the street
against traffic
my mother tongue
cannot be restricted
to one sex
my mother tongue
has never cut its hair
my mother tongue
is primordial
visceral
innate

my mother tongue
shouts
give up the funk!
get your groove on!
express yourself!
my mother tongue
chants
percussive groove
the compelling
restorative, retelling
rhythms of poetry
my mother tongue
joyfully ululates
the very essence
that I am
that I wish to be

now I've stuck out
my tongue
for you
come on
it's your turn
to French me

Champagne Dance

translucent bones
surround the universe
a ribcage of questions
brilliant and old
cartilage of time
and change
white stars drifting
like snow

my brothers
tell me the secret
the one you have kept
from us
for so very long

why did you leave
us behind

prisoners here
rooted to the rhythms
of seas and seasons
mocked
by the perpetual
pinwheel of night

with no rescue
with no escape
but to open the window
of sky
to stare up
into the vast
black winter

to listen
to the ice melting
in our glasses

drunk on eternity

HardDrive/SoftWear

sit you down
on my laptop
baby
make love
to my motherboard
fondle
my mouse
with your slim fingers
make my internet
cry "oh lord!"

plug me
into your USB hub
juice me up
with your
anti-spy
come, applicate me
Facebook and make me
scream! when
the cybersparks fly

oh, link to me
with your hard
drive baby
fill my
inbox
with spurts of
spam
IM me, befriend me
CD-rom, RAM
and send me
with kicks from your
naughty webcam

then download
into my
iPod
baby

lick and remix me
make my pixel count
climb
you know you excite
me when you
megabyte me
so...Google me
anytime!

QRU

I am
in the queue
not quite
at the front
definitely
behind you

I am
in the queue
waiting
my turn
not making noise
but feeling
the burn

I am
in the queue
one step
forward
back
another two

I am
in the queue
pass me
that bottle
for a drink
this will take
a while I think
don't you?

Antiphon for Winter Solstice

—with Dylan Thomas (1914-1953),
Alfred Lord Tennyson (1809-1892),
Percy Bysshe Shelley (1792-1822)

Year flickers to a close,
the days losing light.

A growl fills the trees;
moments later, its bite.

do not go gentle into that good night

Only a fool believes winter
is but barren field—

from snowflake to Milky Way,
Fibonacci revealed.

to strive, to seek, to find, and not to yield

Luminous souls light the way
where the living once shined.

Be fierce—squeeze the fruit,
spike the juice, and garnish with rind.

if winter comes, can spring be far behind?

Flow

get off the fence stop trying to warm up the car and stop trying to catch up on the work just do it tomorrow is only a day away and there's no time to waste yesterday is over gone down the tubes vanished in the wind and today well today is here already and half over forget making more coffee you've had enough forget the phone facebook and being tired wasted cold tagged snowed in disgruntled befriended tomorrow is coming it's only a day away stop looking behind you rejection doesn't care one way or the other and it certainly doesn't matter not in this day and age so hurry up you know what you need to do just do it and don't look back don't ask for trouble don't doubt yourself don't think about it for one second more don't you know tomorrow is only a day away almost on the doorstep forget everything else just focus just do it

Día de los Muertes

Dead will have their day,
And the living, all the
Years before and after.
Ofrendas honor departed
Friends, *familia.* Smile of
The *calavera* along with the
Headiness of marigolds.
Everything in its place:
Dead in their deep sleep,
Estranged from the earth,
And the living, a parade
Dancing their way home.

Pools of–

evening's window

setting sun bleeds
candy-apple copper
into the lake

and I find myself
thinking

the whole world
is a vampire

and it is getting
                    dark

The View

"The mind is not a vessel to be filled but a fire to be kindled."
—Plutarch

Telescope or microscope,
it doesn't matter. The view is the same.
Starcluster colonies, stitched together
in a distant galaxy or under the slide,
begging questions. Being kindling.

Telescope or microscope,
either way we're looking at ourselves.
Starduster colonies stitched together
on this tiny cell of a long stellar arm,
defiant, mystical. Kindled.

Acknowledgments

Grateful acknowledgment is given to the following publications in which these poems first appeared, sometimes in slightly different versions.

If there are two dates listed, the one in parentheses is the year it was written; the second date is the year it was first published.

If the poem is previously unpublished, the date it was written is listed.

Age of Aquarius — (c. 2000) 2009 *HardDrive/SoftWear*
All I Want Is to Leave — (2008) 2012 *Cravings*
Antiphon for Winter Solstice — (2016)
Baby Needs a New Pair of Wings — 2009 *Eviscerator Heaven*
Back That Thang Up — (2013) 2014 *Corpus Lingua*
Back to the Pack — (2008) 2012 *Fortune Cookie*
Bad, Inc. — 2010 *Haggard & Halloo*
BeatStreet Cleveland — (2015)
Black and White — 2006 *Ship of Fools*
Black Mass — 1997 *Ship of Fools*
Blue Heart — 2006 *Nerve Cowboy*
Blue Moon — 1997 (as "Full Moonlight Blues") *B.A.D.* (U. K.)
Bohemian Vendetta — 1996 *Malevolence*
Brother, Can You Spare a Dime — 2011 *Pine Mountain Sand & Gravel*
Bufo Alvarius — (1994)
Butterfly — 2009 *Eviscerator Heaven*
Cary Grant Walks — (1986) 1998 *Ship of Fools*
Casting Call — (2010) 2011 *Braless*
Champagne Dance — (1996)1998 *Malevolence*
Check Out — 2011 *Guerilla Pamphlets*
Cinco de Mayo Moon — (2012) 2013 "Walt's Corner" *The Long Islander*
Cleveland Spelled Backwards Is — 2010 *Deep Cleveland Junkmail Oracle*
Communication Breakdown — (1997) 2009 *HardDrive/SoftWear*
Conscientious Objector — 2012 *Cravings*
Countdown — (2010)
Cravings — 2010 *Vending Machine Poetry for Change* (The Poet's Haven)
Cupid — 2012 *Bad Ink*
Daisy Chain — 2010 *What I Knew Before I Knew* (Pudding House)
Dark Shadow — 1982 *Reflections* (Old House Publishing)
Día de los Muertos — 2015 Poems-For-All #1285
Disco — 2014 EKPHRASTACY (Heights Arts Gallery)
Drumming Circle — 1997 (as "Virgin Stonehenge") *Dasoku: A Journal of Arts and Letters*
Each Stroke a Promise — 2009 *Hessler Street Fair Anthology*
Easter/West — (2011) 2012 *Bad Ink*

Elemental — 1997 *Naturally Magazine*
Everybody Must Get Stoned — (2014)
Family Tree — (2010) 2011 *Braless*
Few Dollar Man — (2009) 2012 *Fortune Cookie*
Fire — (2012)
Flow — (2009) 2010 (as "Flux Redux") *Braless*
Flower Power — (2014) 2015 *Hessler Street Fair Anthology*
Fortune Cookie — (2010) 2012 *Fortune Cookie*
Frankie's Too Cool — (2010) 2012 *Fortune Cookie*
Frank Sinatra Sighs — (1998) 2006 *Ship of Fools*
Fusion — 1996 *Ship of Fools*
Going Braless — (2010) 2011 *Braless*
Got Soul? — (2011) 2012 *Fortune Cookie*
Greenheart — (1998) 2008 *Hessler Street Fair Anthology*
Hairy Situation — (2013) 2014 *Corpus Lingua*
Happy Hour — 2013 *While You Were Sleeping I Dreamt a Poem*
(Kattywompus Press)
HardDrive/SoftWear — 2009 RTA Cleveland
Her First Time — 2002 *Rosebud*
Hipster — (2013) 2014 *Corpus Lingua*
Hippie Chick, Baby — (2013) 2014 *Corpus Lingua*
Import — (2010*)* 2012 *Fortune Cookie*
In a Bar, the Basement, a Microphone, and Poets — (2016) 2016
Hessler Street Fair Anthology
Incontinence — (2010) 2012 *Fortune Cookie*
In This Desert — (1986) 1999 *juju*, Belfast, Ireland
Jawbone — (2010) 2012 *Fortune Cookie*
Kicking It — (2010) 2011 *Braless*
Learning the Form — (2010) 2012 *Fortune Cookie*
Let's Get It On — 2015 *Thunderclap Amen*
Licking Winter — 2006 *Ship of Fools*
Lost — 1995 *Ship of Fools*
Lovechild — 1994 *Ship of Fools*
Making Scents — (2009) 2010 *Hessler Street Fair Anthology*
Merrily, Merrily — 2009 *HardDrive/SoftWear*
Mother Tongue — (2014) 2015 *Thunderclap Amen*
Mutability — (2011) 2012 *Cravings*
NetWork — (2010) 2011 *Braless*
Night Ballet — 1999 *Ship of Fools*
One Peachy Day — (1996) 1997 *The Magnetic Poetry® Book of
Poetry* (Workman Publishing)
One Small Step — 2011 *Crisis Chronicles Cyber Litmag*
Pink Hell — (2007) 2008 *Slipstream*
Pools of- — 1994 *Ship of Fools*, 1996 *Voices of Cleveland* (CSU)
Psalm — 2007 *Ship of Fools*
Purdah — (1996) 1998 *Nerve Cowboy*
QRU — (2011) 2012 *Cravings*
Reading Palms — (2013) 2014 *Corpus Lingua*
Red Stilettos — (2010) 2011 *Braless*
Rocker — (2012) 2014 *rendezvous* (Society for the Dissemination of

Art)
Sacrifice & Broken Fevers — (1996) 1997 *The Magnetic Poetry® Book of Poetry* (Workman Publishing)
Seeds — 2013 *Vending Machine Poetry for Change* (The Poet's Haven)
Serious Flannel — (2010) 2011 *Braless*
Serious Moonlight* — 2016 *The Stars Look Very Different Today – A David Bowie Tribute* (Poems-For-All #1413)
Soul Custody — (2006) 2008 *Ship of Fools*
Stopping by Bar on a Rainy Evening — 2009 *Mnemosyne*
Story Book — 2009 (with different formatting) *Ship of Fools*
Sugar, Spice and Everything Twice — (2011) 2012 *Bad Ink*
Summer and Smoke — 1998 *Nerve Cowboy*
Thaumaturgy — (2010) 2011 *Rosebud*
The Nightmare Spinners — (2006)
These Places — 1997 *Libido: The Journal of Sex and Sensibility*
The View — (2014) 2015 *Great Lakes Review*
Thirst — 2012 *Cravings*
Tie-Dye — 1997 *Iota* (U.K.)
Tribe — (2014) 2015 *Great Lakes Review*
Trick Whore Treat — (2009) 2012 *Bad Ink*
Two Bottles — (2010) 2011 *Braless*
Water — (2012)
Wet — 2010 *Project Water* (Amy Mothersbaugh's Studio 2091)
When October's Throat Is Cut to Celebrate Samhain — 1995 *Ship of Fools*
Where the Sky Goes — (2006) 2010 *Speak Peace: American Voices Respond to Vietnamese Children's Paintings* (Wick Poetry Center)
Wood I Love You — (2009)
Wraiths — 1987 *Blue Unicorn*
You Are You — 2012 *Cravings*

*some lines from this poem also appeared in the poem "First Kiss" — (1996) 2014 *We Only Come Out at Night* (The Poet's Haven)

HardDrive/SoftWear – Crisis Chronicles Press
Braless – Blasted Press
Cravings – recycled karma press
Bad Ink – Writing Knights Press
Fortune Cookie – Kattywompus Press
Corpus Lingua – The Poet's Haven
Thunderclap Amen – Crisis Chronicles Press

Cover art for *Age of Aquarius* by Camren (10 May 2015), art property of John & Geri Burroughs, used with permission

JOHN B. BURROUGHS
EDITOR / PUBLISHER / POET
JC@CRISISCHRONICLES.COM

3431 GEORGE AVENUE
PARMA, OH 44134 USA
WWW.CRISISCHRONICLES.COM
TWITTER @JESUSCRISIS
(440) 315-0426

CRISIS CHRONICLES PRESS
VITAL INDEPENDENT LITERATURE SINCE 2008
CCPRESS.BLOGSPOT.COM   FACEBOOK.COM/CRISISCHRONICLESPRESS